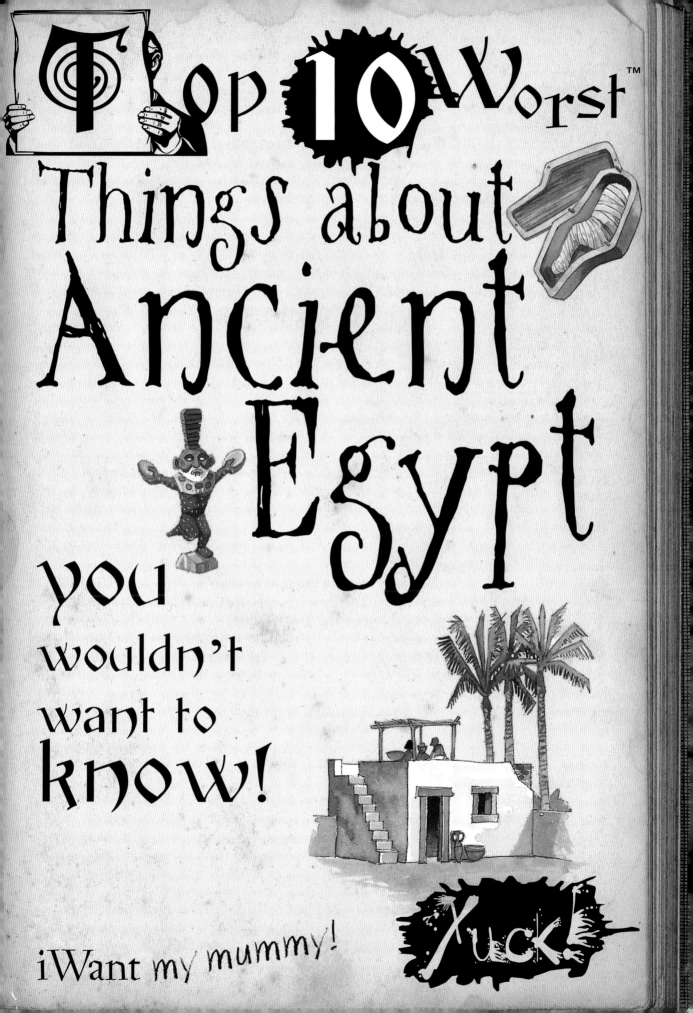

# Top 10 Worst Things about Ancient Egypt

## you wouldn't want to know!

iWant my mummy!

Yuck!

*Author:*
Victoria England was born in Bath, England. She
studied English Literature at the University of
Brighton and now lives and works in Brighton.

*Artist:*
David Antram was born in Brighton, England, in
1958. He studied at Eastbourne College of Art and
then worked in advertising for fifteen years before
becoming a full-time artist. He has illustrated many
children's non-fiction books.

*Series creator:*
David Salariya was born in Dundee, Scotland.
He has illustrated a wide range of books and has
created and designed many new series for
publishers in the UK and overseas. In 1989 he
established The Salariya Book Company. He lives
in Brighton with his wife, illustrator Shirley Willis,
and their son Jonathan.

*Additional artwork:* John James

*Editorial assistants:* Rob Walker, Mark Williams

Published in Great Britain in MMXII by
Book House, an imprint of
**The Salariya Book Company Ltd**
25 Marlborough Place, Brighton BN1 1UB
www.salariya.com
www.book-house.co.uk

HB ISBN-13: 978-1-908177-22-3
PB ISBN-13: 978-1-908177-23-0

# SALARIYA

1 3 5 7 9 8 6 4 2
A CIP catalogue record for this book is available
from the British Library.

Printed and bound in China.

PAPER FROM
SUSTAINABLE
FORESTS

@bookhousebooks  The Salariya  BookHouse100
Book Company

FIND OUR BOOKS
ON THE APP STORE:
SEARCH FOR 'SALARIYA'

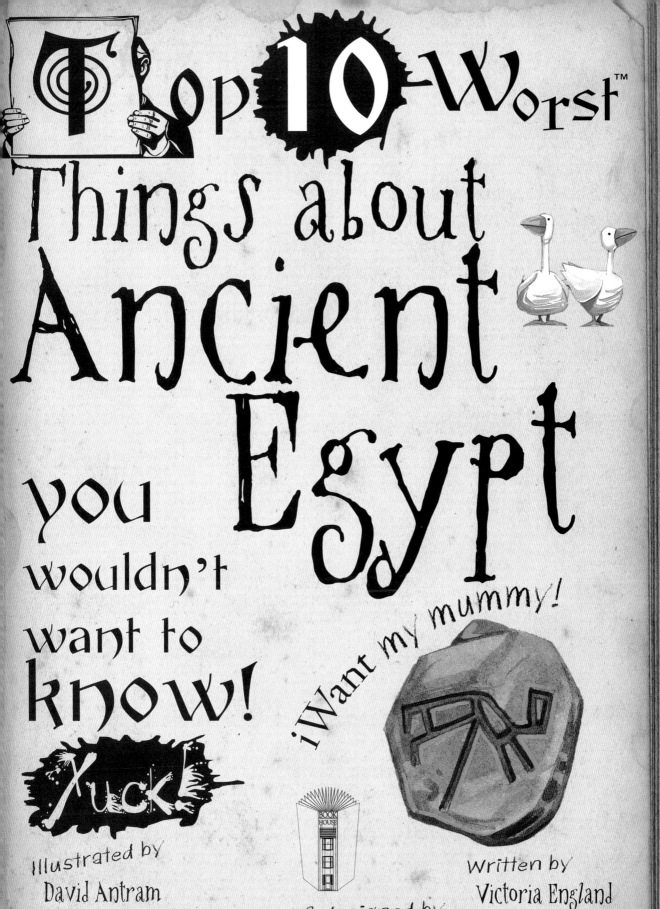

# Top 10 Worst Things about Ancient Egypt you wouldn't want to know!

Yuck!

iWant my mummy!

Illustrated by
David Antram

BOOK HOUSE

Created & designed by
David Salariya

Written by
Victoria England

# Contents

# Where in the world?

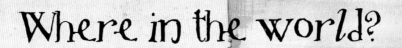

**E**gypt was one of the greatest civilisations of the past. The monuments and tombs of their pharaohs remain intact today, some 4,000 years later!

Situated in the north-east corner of Africa, the River Nile runs through the country into the Mediterranean Sea. Every year, its banks overflowed and flooded a strip of land a few kilometres wide. This is the area coloured green on the map. Without this flood watering the soil, Egypt would be made up entirely of stone-dry desert.

For the most part ancient Egypt was a prosperous and enjoyable place to live, but what were the worst things about living as an ancient Egyptian?

MEDITERRANEAN SEA

Delta

Memphis

River Nile

Akhetaten
(El-Almarna)

Valley of the Kings • • Thebes

*The silt left by the flood was rich, fertile land and is shown on the map in green.*

# Life and death in ancient Egypt

Although ancient Egyptian history spans 30 centuries, the lives of ordinary people hardly changed at all. They used the same tools, farmed in the same way, wore similar clothes and had mostly the same beliefs. They thought their way of life was the right way, and saw no reason for change.

*If peasants were too poor to own an ox, they dug the land by hand.*

huff!  puff!

## Egyptian landscape

The land was hot and parched. People relied on the Nile for water. Beyond the fertile land on either side of the river stretched the desert. In the spring, hot winds blew from it, bringing blistering sandstorms. For ancient Egyptians the desert was an enemy.

# Water is life

The river gave life, not only to humans but to lots of wild creatures. Its waters were full of fish, many of which were delicious to eat, like the grey mullet and Nile perch. The papyrus reeds of the delta and other marshy stretches teemed with bird life – ducks, teal, crane, quail and ibis.

# Wildlife & plants

The desert was the home of lions, jackals, antelope, gazelle and ibex. Very little grew apart from thorn trees. In contrast, the Nile valley was green with crops and shade-giving trees. The most common trees were the date palm, the dom-palm, which has a nut-like fruit, and the sycamore fig.

*Lotus-flower stern*

*An Egyptian cargo boat, with a stern shaped like a lotus flower, has lowered sail, ready to unload. Because of its size its hull needs to be braced by a long rope.*

# Taming the Nile

Everything the farmers grew depended on the Nile. Dykes prevented the flood water from draining away and canals took it to the farmers' fields. Careless landowners who let their canals leak robbed other people of water. One of the most important departments of the king's government would oversee the sharing of water along more than 100 kilometres of river.

# Dangers and death

The ancient Egyptians dreaded evil spirits and believed that most misfortunes were caused by them. The average age of death was probably around 36 years, although many people lived much longer. The pharaoh Pepi II ruled for 94 years, the longest reign we know of in history.

7

# Daily life in ancient Egypt

Horus

Thoth

Osiris

Ra

Isis

Hathor

Anubis

The gods played a large part in the lives of the ancient Egyptians. They liked great festivals to be held in their honour, which the people also enjoyed. Pharaohs also created huge temples for the gods, as monuments to be remembered by.

## Towns & villages

The towns were protected by a wall with a gate that was guarded by day and shut at night. On the east bank there were large cities, but not on the west. That was where the dead were buried. The ancient Egyptians believed that the dead travelled into the west and, like the sun, they would wake to a new life.

# Rich & poor

*Wages came in various useful forms such as grain, oil or fine linen cloth.*

Rich families could look forward to a pleasant life, with servants to wait on them and free time to enjoy themselves. But there were far more poor families than rich in ancient Egypt. People did not think this was unjust. They accepted that some people were born to work, and others could tell them what to do.

# Neighbours

The ancient Egyptians were not interested in seeing how foreigners lived, or travelling to their lands. They thought that people beyond their borders were very unfortunate to live in lands so much less pleasant than Egypt. They did not like foreign clothes or habits either, and thought they were unclean.

*Tutankhamun became pharaoh when he was only nine years old.*

# The pharaoh

The Egyptians believed that each king of Egypt was a living god. The king was given the title *pharaoh*, which means 'great house'. The pharaoh used local governors and huge numbers of officials to carry out his orders.

*The Pharaoh's ring was his official stamp used to mark documents containing his orders.*

# No 10

## Tradition

Ancient Egyptians had very set ways of doing things. Each important stage of life – birth, marriage and death – had to be approached in a certain way. It was taken for granted that old people were wiser than young people, for they had had much more time in which to learn. Egyptians would not have understood the notion that by taking a fresh look at things people could have made new discoveries about the world.

### Giving birth

Waahhh!

A birth stool was a low platform with a central hole on which women squatted to give birth. Most babies were born this way.

*Children were meant to do as they were told and were not encouraged to have ideas of their own.*

puff!  huff!

# Be prepared!
## Always expect the very worst

### Marriage

In ancient Egypt people could decide whom they wished to marry, although elders would be expected to introduce suitable couples to each other. If a wife was ill-treated by her husband she could appeal to a judge for help. The judge would then tell the husband to improve his behaviour, but if his cruelty continued he would receive a hundred lashes!

### Childhood

Only children of rich parents were sent to school, so most poor people could not read or write. In school they learnt by copying and chanting wisdom texts which gave advice on morals and behaviour. The schools can't have been very pleasant places to be, as the children were regularly beaten. One scribe wrote:

*'The ears of a boy are in his back. He listens only when he is beaten.'*

### Death

At Egyptian funerals the mummy, in a mummy-shaped coffin, was drawn along on a sledge. A priest performed the Opening of the Mouth ceremony (above), which brought the senses to life again. Priests then took the mummy to its underground tomb where a stone coffin case would be ready for it.

*Priests, courtiers and servants followed the coffin.*

11

# № 9

# Dressing the part

Ancient Egyptians took a lot of care over their appearance. Egyptian clothes hardly altered over hundreds of years, so they could not dress to impress by wearing a new style. Instead, people took pride in keeping themselves and their clothes spotlessly clean and neatly arranged at all times.

*Wealthy people could stay cool and fresh in a robe of the thinnest linen, sashed with a huge pleated belt. The linen was extremely expensive.*

## Making linen

Clothes were almost always made of linen, which was woven from fibres of the flax plant. Flax was harvested by being pulled out of the ground, not cut. This back-breaking work was done mostly by men. The stems were soaked for several days to separate the fibres which were then beaten until they were soft. The spinner fixed the fibres to a spindle and twisted them into a strong thread as she let the spindle drop.

*Twisting the spindle*

*Weaving on a loom*

# Be prepared!
## Always expect the very worst

### Bath time

After bathing, ancient Egyptians rubbed themselves with scented oils and draped themselves in fine linen.

*The perfumed oils helped to protect the ancient Egyptians from the sun and the dry heat.*

### Getting dressed

Workers wore practical loincloths or simple tunic dresses. People often worked naked; servant girls sometimes wore just a belt. Wealthy people wore wide garments of transparent white linen, which were pleated, draped and tied. Some Egyptian women had henna tattoos on their arms, legs and stomach, but tattoos weren't worn by noble women so these were best avoided!

### A close shave

Priests followed strict rules of cleanliness. They had to wash several times a day, and shave their head. All body hair was removed in order to be pure enough to approach the god, so it was either shaved or plucked out with tweezers. Priests were not allowed to wear wool or leather sandals, as sheep and goats were thought to be unclean.

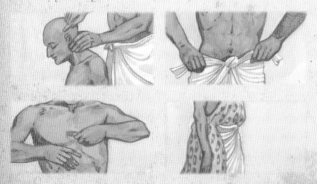

### Dress to impress

Rich people did not show their wealth by wearing gorgeously patterned clothes or exaggerated styles. They wore the finest transparent white linen gauze, which was very expensive as everyone knew, and they hung fortunes around their necks in the form of gold necklaces set with turquoise and lapis lazuli.

*Women wore powdered mineral colours and wigs made from human hair.*

# No 3

## Home comforts

This is the kind of house that working people, neither especially rich nor poor, lived in. It was joined to other houses on either side, and similar houses lined both sides of the street. Some town houses were two or three storeys high. In poorer parts these would often have been crammed with several families. There was a shortage of land for town houses, because nobody wanted to live in the desert and the fertile land near the river was needed for growing food.

## Giant statues

Ancient Egyptians are more famous for their monuments than their houses. Giant statues of the pharaoh adorned temples which were attached to the pyramid. 172 men were needed to haul each statue.

*Rats gnawed holes in the walls of the houses and there was a high risk of flooding.*

*Kitchen*

*Bedroom and storeroom*

*Vent for light and air*

# Be prepared!
## Always expect the very worst

## In the home

The houses would have seemed bare to us, with just a few stools and some small tables on which dishes and drinking vessels could be placed for meals. There were no cupboards, so possessions were kept in wooden chests, baskets and jars. An ordinary family might have only one bed, or none. People would sleep on mats on the floor or the roof, although the danger from scorpions made them use a headrest.

## Protecting the home

One room was fitted with an altar in a shrine-like enclosure, for family worship of a friendly household god, such as Bes or Tauert. Ancient Egyptians believed that Bes would protect their home and keep away evil spirits.

*Bes*

*Often peasant homes had only one room which all the family shared.*

There's too much sand in this bread!

Hrmph!

Grumble

15

# No 7

## food and famine

In very poor families, the diet of bread, beans, onions and green vegetables would have probably become extremely boring. The really poor lived on boiled papyrus roots. Many exotic fruits that we enjoy today, such as lemons and cherries, were unknown.

### Tomb offerings

It was the duty of relatives to visit tombs with gifts of food so that the dead person did not go hungry in the afterlife. In a nobleman's tomb at Saqqarah researchers found a whole meal, consisting of barley porridge, quail, kidneys, pigeon stew, fish, a rib of beef, bread and figs.

*Sometimes meat was embalmed for people to enjoy in the afterlife.*

### Nice to meat you

Egyptians enjoyed beef most, if they could afford it. It was expensive because cattle needed fields of grass to eat and that took up precious land. People thought that mutton and goat were not so good, and pork and fish were considered unclean.

Gulp!

# Be prepared!
## Always expect the very worst

## How to make fire

It took a bow-drill, a piece of wood with a row of holes, and a hard stick that just fitted into them. The stick was pressed into a hole and rotated fast with the drill. As the wood rubbed together, a spark was produced.

**Owww!**

## Worn gnashers

Most Egyptians had terrible teeth, as sand from the desert got into their bread and ground their teeth down. The Egyptians cleaned their teeth with toothbrushes made from twigs and toothpaste made from natron, a natural salt found on the shores of the desert lakes.

## What did the wealthy eat?

Even prosperous peasants had their own vegetable patches. Pigeons, crane, teal, geese and ducks were reared for eating and food was forced into some birds to fatten them. Food was bought at the local market where country people sold what they did not need for themselves. As well as growing and buying, people hunted and fished for food; this was a way for poor people to get delicacies.

**Delicious!**

*Dinner-party plates were encrusted with jewels.*

# No 6

## Extreme sports

Hunting for wild animals such as hippos, crocodiles, elephants, lions and rhinos was fun, but also extremely dangerous. Hunting expeditions with the pharaohs often resembled military campaigns more than pleasure outings. When big-game hunting, the king was accompanied by soldiers wearing full military gear, as was the king himself in his chariot.

### Riding a chariot

Hunting in the desert with chariots was only for the very wealthy. Tutankhamun's bow was inscribed with two hieroglyphs meaning 'possessor of a strong arm.'

# Be prepared!
# Always expect the very worst

## Let's play senet!

*Hmmm...*

*Senet was a game played on a rectangular board divided into squares. Casting-sticks were used to see who got the highest score.*

## Pets

In ancient Egyptian times dogs probably looked like greyhounds. When a cat died, members of the family would shave off their eyebrows as a sign of mourning. The goose was not a household pet, but some people let it wander into their houses because it was sacred to the wind god, Amun. A wealthy family may have kept a monkey as an amusing pet, but keeping it under control was a job for the servants!

*Honk!*

## Festivals

The festival of the local god was a great event of the year for everyone. Priests acted out plays showing the god's deeds, and a huge procession with singers, dancers and music filled the streets. The gloomiest festival was in the fourth month, when Egypt went into mourning for the death of the god Osiris.

*More wine?*

# No 5

# Gods, dreams and curses

*The hawk-headed sun god Ra.*

**E**gypt was a prosperous land with few powerful enemies. People were more anxious about the threat of danger from the gods. They thought Seth, the cruel red god of the desert, was the cause of most troubles. There was also the chance that normally well-disposed gods might be offended if they felt neglected.

When the Gods were angry:

*The Nile didn't rise enough at flood time, so crops couldn't grow and people starved.*

*Swarms of locusts (flying insects that gobble up crops) descended on the fields and ruined the harvest.*

## Animal gods

Egyptians worshipped animals such as baboons, crocodiles and cats. A Roman visitor was once stoned to death for accidentally killing a cat!

Baloon    Cat    Crocodile

Before / After

Snap!

*A crocodile could upset boats while fishing on the Nile. Yikes!*

# Be prepared!
# Always expect the very worst

## The power of magic

People were very superstitious in the ancient world. The Egyptians used spells to solve their everyday problems, and curses to bring bad luck to their enemies. For them, magic called *heka* was a good thing. They believed it helped to create the world and kept the universe going by guiding the sun god's boat through the underworld.

## Temples of the gods

Ancient Egyptians believed that everything that happened in the world was controlled by the gods, so it was most important not to offend them. Every town had several large temples and each one was the home of a god. Each pharaoh tried to outdo previous ones by building an even more enormous temple; ordinary people were not allowed inside.

## Dreams

People believed that dreams had meanings:

- If you dream someone gives you white bread, you will be lucky.

- Having a dream that your teeth are falling out is a warning of the death of someone very near to you.

- To dream that you have the face of a leopard is a very good omen and you will become an important leader.

Uh~oh!

Ra          Osiris          Isis          Anubis          Horus          Thoth

# No 4

# Deadly diseases

**L**ife expectancy in ancient Egypt was lower than in many modern populations (as we saw on page 7). Whilst some ancient Egyptians undoubtedly enjoyed long lives, most were unlikely to live beyond about 36 years of age. Many mummies have been discovered with signs of disease or injury. Herbs played an important part in Egyptian medicine, along with minerals and animal products.

## Amulets

In order to prevent illness, ancient Egyptians carried amulets – lucky charms which gave protection against the evil spirits that cause disease. The eye of Horus was a particularly powerful sign to ward off sickness and misfortune.

*Some temples had accommodation for the very sick who were hoping for a miraculous cure. They prayed and received treatment from the priests.*

Bleurgh!

# Be prepared!
## Always expect the very worst

*Ancient Egyptian doctors were good at setting fractures.*

## Off-colour days

Some days of the year were thought to be very unlucky, as evil forces were particularly strong. On these days it was best to avoid bathing, making a journey, killing an ox, a goat or a duck, lighting a fire in a house, or eating anything that lives in water.

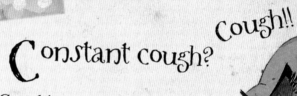

## Constant cough?

Coughing and lung diseases were both common. Incurable breathing problems were caused by inhaling sand during sandstorms. Coughing could be a sign of parasitic worms in the lungs. A longer sort of worm could also end up in the arms and legs and needed to be wound out on a stick. Ouch!

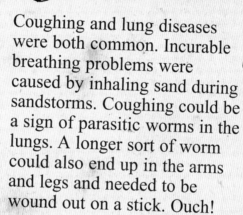

Pull!

Cough!!

Cough!!

## That's magic!

Oww!

The ancient Egyptians thought that all misfortunes without an obvious external cause were sent by evil spirits. It was therefore quite logical for doctors to recite spells over their patients. It wasn't all magic, though. Some of the earliest medical and surgical records have been found in Egypt. One of the earliest is the Ebers Papyrus, written about 1550 BC, which lists 700 cures for common sicknesses and problems.

*Apart from pulling out the tooth, there was nothing that could be done for toothache.*

23

# No 3

# Crime and punishment

No-one was more important than the pharaoh. His Egyptian subjects were anxious for his welfare and keen to obey him. He was all-powerful, all-knowing, and ruled everyone's fate. He ruled the government and law courts, was chief priest of the temples, headed the army and controlled trade, irrigation, mines and granaries.

## Ask the statue

If a crime couldn't be proven in court, the victim could appeal to a local god when its statue was paraded through town. They could call out their problem to the statue – 'Lord, who stole my ox?' or, 'Who has moved my boundary stones?' and the statue might nod at the thief's door.

## A taxing time

Ancient Egyptians had to put up with the tax men who measured crops, checked on work and noted what people must pay. However, there was a way to make life easier: bribes often made tax inspectors or law-court officers much more friendly and helpful.

## Punishments

Beating was the most common punishment. Slaves, servants and hard-up taxpayers were beaten as much as their punishers liked, but if a court ordered a beating, the weapon and the number of blows would be stated.

### smack!

# Be prepared!
## Always expect the very worst

### Tomb robbery!

Every Egyptian pharaoh and his officials feared that the treasures in their tomb would be targeted by robbers. And they were right: few tombs escaped this unwanted attention. Robbers ripped open the mummies, looking for treasure, so they often had to be re-wrapped, sometimes gaining extra heads or legs in the process!

*The penalty for tomb robbing was torture and then a slow and painful death by impalement.*

*Hieroglyph for impalement*

### What were they looking for?

- Linen was extremely valuable because of the time it took to weave the smallest amount. It could also be re-used.

- Glass was scarce in ancient Egypt. Since it could be melted down and made into new objects, stolen glass could not be traced.

- Gold from jewellery was prized and melted down to re-use.

- Frankincense and myrrh were highly prized because of their fragrance and their use in the art of mummification.

# No 2

## Hard labour

Heave-ho!

Most people in ancient Egypt faced a life of hard work. The pharaoh sent officials around the villages to call people up to build pyramids. It took 20 years and a workforce of 4,000 to build one stone pyramid. The men worked from sunrise to sunset, slept in crowded barracks and only got one day off in ten. There was no machinery, so workers had to haul the building materials manually and were often involved in serious accidents.

### The pyramid of power

Here is an overview of the power structure in ancient Egypt, with the most powerful at the top:

**The Pharaoh**
The Great Royal Wife
Members of the Royal Family
The Vizier
Noblemen
Army Officers
Court Officials
Priests and Priestesses, Doctors
Scribes and Teachers
Artists
Craftsmen
Foot Soldiers
Fishermen and Farmers
Labourers, Tomb Builders

Ouch!

# Be prepared!
# Always expect the very worst

## Sent to the quarries

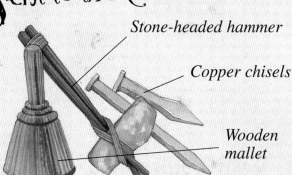

Stone-headed hammer

Copper chisels

Wooden mallet

Most workers sent to quarries would be working underground, as the best stone was beneath the surface. It was backbreaking work, but not as grim as being sent to quarry granite in the far south of Egypt. It was boiling hot there and workers would be out in the open, trying to cut into very hard rock with a lump of stone.

## Working on the farm

Some people in Egypt were very rich – the pharaoh and his court, high-ranking officials and wealthy landowners – but the majority were poor. Some made a living by making things to sell, especially in the towns, but most people earned their keep by farming the land. Ordinary Egyptians grew crops for rich landowners; in return they were allowed a patch of land to grow things to feed their own family.

Careful! Careful!

## Scraping a living

For eight months farmers were hard at it, ploughing, sowing, weeding, watering (it hardly ever rained) and harvesting. Then the Nile flood came and for the rest of the year they couldn't farm, because the land was under water.

Mattock

# No 1

# Mummification

The ancient Egyptians took a lot of trouble getting ready for life in the next world. Those who could afford to do so made elaborate preparations. Ordering a tomb built of stone was the first step. All wealthy people did this long before they expected to die. They might also arrange the details of their own mummification, to make sure they were given the best.

## Gory mummification

The brain was removed first, pulled out through the nostrils with an iron hook. Then a long cut was made on the left side of the body through which all the internal organs were removed.

Urgh!

Boo!

*A priest dressed as the god Anubis supervised the wrapping.*

# Be prepared!
## Always expect the very worst

### Get stuffed!

The heart was left inside the body which was then put in natron to dry out for 100 days. After this, the skin was shrivelled and wrinkled and the body looked like a piece of old leather. The empty space where the organs were was filled with sawdust, rags and chaff. False eyes were made out of onions and sometimes false hair was made from string.

### Canopic jars

The canopic jar with the head of the god Imsety contained the liver.

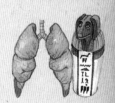

The jar with the jackal head of Duamutef contained the stomach.

The intestines were put in the jar topped with the hawk head of the god Qebehsenuef.

The jar topped with the god Hapy contained the lungs.

### Making the mummy

It took 15 days and 20 layers of linen bandages to wrap up the mummy. Resin was used to glue the bandages together. Linen pads were placed between the bandages to give a good rounded shape. Once completely wrapped in bandages, the mummy was placed in two special large shrouds secured with linen strips.

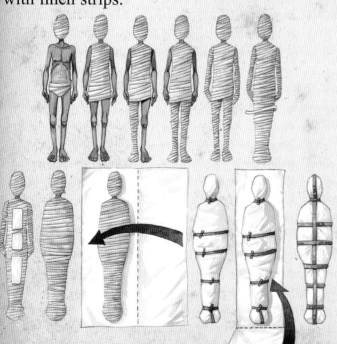

### In the afterlife

In death non-royals were judged before Osiris and their hearts weighed against the Feather of Truth. If found free from sin, the deceased would be admitted to the realms of the dead. The monster Ammut (a combination of crocodile, lion and hippo) waited in the judgement hall to eat the hearts of those that failed the test.

# Glossary

**Amulet** A small object, either worn or carried, which was thought to ward off evil.

**Bow-drill** A drill worked by a string and a small bow. When the bow was pushed backwards and forwards the string made the drill rotate.

**Chaff** Dust made from the outer husks of grain, produced by threshing.

**Dyke** A long wall or embankment built to prevent flooding from the sea.

**Embalming** A process in which fluids are removed from a dead body and replaced with chemicals that prevent decay.

**Flax** A plant from which linen is made.

**Gauze** A very thin transparent fabric.

**Granary** A building in which grain is stored.

**Granite** A very hard rock formed mostly of the minerals quartz and feldspar.

**Henna** A tree or shrub with fragrant white or reddish flowers. A reddish-orange dye can be prepared from the dried and ground leaves.

**Hieroglyphs** Symbols used in the sacred writings of ancient Egypt.

**Ibex** A wild goat, found in mountainous areas of Europe, northern Africa and Asia.

**Ibis** A bird related to the heron.

**Irrigation** The watering of the land by artificial means, such as the digging of canals.

**Lapis lazuli** A dark blue semi-precious stone.

**Loincloth** A strip of cloth worn around the waist.

**Loom** An apparatus for making thread or yarn into cloth by weaving strands together.

**Lower Egypt** The Nile valley from the Mediterranean Sea to Cairo.

**Mattock** A digging tool, with a blade at right angles to the handle.

**Natron** A form of soda, found in the ground in some parts of the world.

**Osiris** God of death and rebirth. According to legend, he was a king killed by his evil brother, Seth. His wife, Isis, put his body back together, to make the first mummy, and Osiris was reborn as a god.

**Papyrus** A reed growing beside the Nile, used to make paper.

**Parasite** A small creature that feeds from a larger creature and relies on it to stay alive.

**Pharaoh** An Egyptian king. Traditionally the pharaoh was a man, but a woman could also rule.

**Resin** Sap that oozes from the trunks of some pine and fir trees.

**Saqqarah** A vast ancient burial ground in Egypt.

**Scribe** A professional writer. Most officials were trained as scribes.

**Shrine** A cupboard-like container in which the image of a god is kept.

**Shroud** A cloth in which a body is wrapped for burial.

**Silt** Very fine soil deposited on land when a river floods.

**Spindle** A rod or pin, tapered at one end and usually weighted at the other, on which fibres are spun into thread by hand and then wound.

**Temple** A building dedicated to religious ceremonies or worship; home to priests, scribes and officials.

**Thresh** To beat or trample grain crops in order to separate the grain from the husks and straw.

**Underworld** A place beneath the earth, which the ancient Egyptians believed was full of hidden dangers. After death, they had to find their way through the underworld safely, with the help of spells and prayers, before they could enter the afterlife.

**Upper Egypt** The Nile valley roughly from Cairo in the north to Aswan in the south.

**Vizier** A ruler's chief minister.

# Top 10 Worst things about Ancient Egypt

## Index

## Cherished Library

David Arscott
HB ISBN: 978-1-907184-78-9

Jim Pipe
HB ISBN: 978-1-907184-87-1

David Arscott
HB ISBN: 978-1-907184-18-5

David Arscott
HB ISBN: 978-1-907184-25-3

Jim Pipe
HB ISBN: 978-1-907184-26-0

Antony Mason
HB ISBN: 978-1-907184-77-2

Jim Pipe
HB ISBN: 978-1-907184-58-1

Fiona Macdonald
HB ISBN: 978-1-907184-49-9

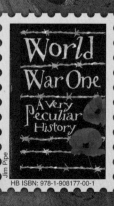

Jim Pipe
HB ISBN: 978-1-908177-00-1

Jacqueline Morley
HB ISBN: 978-1-907184-48-2

Daniel Defoe/Penko Gelev
PB ISBN: 978-906714-75-8

Charles Dickens/Penko Gelev
PB ISBN: 978-1-906714-77-2

William Shakespeare/Penko Gelev
PB ISBN: 978-1-906714-72-7

Charles Dickens/Penko Gelev
PB ISBN: 978-1-906714-76-5

Homer/Li Sidong
PB ISBN: 978-1-906714-37-6

William Shakespeare/Penko Gelev
PB ISBN: 978-1-906714-70-3

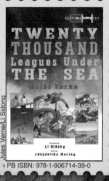

Jules Verne/Li Sidong
PB ISBN: 978-1-906714-39-0

Jonathan Swift/Penko Gelev
PB ISBN: 978-1-906714-38-3

William Shakespeare/Penko Gelev
PB ISBN: 978-1-906714-40-6

Anon/Li Sidong
PB ISBN: 978-1-906714-73-4